Gran Canaria Travel Guide

Attractions, Eating, Drinking, Shopping & Places To Stay

Steve Jonas

Copyright © 2014, Astute Press
All Rights Reserved.

No part of this publication may be reproduced, stored in a retrieval system, or transmitted, in any form or by any means without the prior written permission of the publisher, nor be otherwise circulated in any form of binding or cover other than that in which it is published and without similar condition being imposed on the subsequent purchaser.

If there are any errors or omissions in copyright acknowledgements the publisher will be pleased to insert the appropriate acknowledgement in any subsequent printing of this publication.

Although we have taken all reasonable care in researching this book we make no warranty about the accuracy or completeness of its content and disclaim all liability arising from its use

Table of Contents

Welcome to Gran Canaria 6

Planning Your Stay 11

Climate & Weather 11

Sightseeing 13
  Maspalomas 13
    Lighthouse (El Faro) 13
    Botanical Park (El Parque Botanico) 14
    Banana Park 14
    Holiday World 15
    Aqualand 16
    Palmitos Park 16
  Playa del Ingles 17
    Nightlife 18
  Las Palmas 20
    Playa de las Canteras 21
    Vegueta 22
    Casa de Colon 23
    Triana 24
    Cenobia de Valeron (Valeron Monastery) 26
    Mundo Aborigen (Aborigine World) 27
    Caldera de Bandama 28
    Gran Canaria Carnival 29
  Arucas 30
    Iglesia de San Juan Bautista 31
    Arehucas Rum Distillery 32
  Sioux City, Bahia Feliz 32
  La Cumbre 33
  Telde 34
  Ingenio 35
  Puerto Mogan 36
    Aloe Vera Museum 37
  Puerto Rico 38

Angry Birds Theme Park..38
Galdar **39**
Painted Cave (La Cueva Pintada de Gáldar) 40
Surfing **40**
Crocodile Park **41**
Camel Park, Arteara **42**
Diving in Gran Canaria **43**
Cactualdea (Cactus Park) **44**
Museo del Castillo de la Fortaleza **45**

Places to Stay 46
Cordial Mogan Valle, Puerto Mogan....................................**46**
AC Hotel Gran Canaria Marriott **47**
Club Hotel Riu Gran Canaria...**48**
Hotel Terraza Amadores **48**
Riu Palace Maspalomas...**49**

Eating & Drinking 50
Restaurante La Tapita-Los Jose's, Maspalomas **50**
Mama Mia, Playa del Ingles..**51**
La Oliva, Las Palmas **51**
Amadores Beach Club Restaurant, Puerto Rico **51**
Fusion Restaurant & Lounge Bar, Arguineguin **52**

Shopping 53
Calle Mayor de Triana, Las Palmas **53**
El Muelle Shopping Center (Centro Commercial El Muelle) **53**
Avenida Mesa y Lopez, Las Palmas......................................**54**
FEDAC, Playa del Ingles..**54**
Pueblo Canario (Canarian Village).......................................**55**

Welcome to Gran Canaria

Gran Canaria is the third largest island in the Canary Islands (after Tenerife and Fuerteventura) and has the archipelago's largest population. It's often described as a "miniature continent" because of the variety it offers.

The capital Las Palmas de Gran Canaria is in the northeastern region of Gran Canaria and is one of the largest cities in all of Spain. The south coast features the main tourist towns of the island including the upscale Maspalomas and the British-cultured Playa del Ingles. The centre of the island features a mountainous terrain with picturesque, forested mountain-tops.

If you are looking for a vacation filled with sunbathing and swimming, Gran Canaria will prove to be an excellent holiday destination. Go to Maspalomas in the south of the island, and you will find beaches that stretch for 8 kilometers as well as an impressive landscape of sand dunes.

The capital city of Las Palmas includes Playa de las Canteras, the most popular beach on the Gran Canaria. The golden sand beach is three kilometers long and has a delightful promenade. A 200 meter long reef shelters the beach from the waves and creates a natural lagoon that offers safe swimming.

You can combine shopping, sightseeing, eating and drinking, at El Muelle shopping center in Las Palmas. Overlooking the Puerto de la Luz harbor, the mall is one of the best shopping centers in Spain with 60 shops, open-air disco (5,000 square meters in size), and many other amenities.

If you are interested in water sports like windsurfing and kitesurfing, a number of beach resorts in Gran Canaria will perfectly suit your needs. Those who like the outdoors will learn that the island has some species of plants not seen anywhere else in the world. About half of Gran Canaria has been named a protected biosphere reserve by UNESCO.

Gran Canaria has been a popular spa destination since the 19th century when wealthy European visitors were drawn to Azuaje, located in the Doramas forest and Los Berrazales, which was famed for the healing powers of its iron-rich spring waters. Even before this time, the island's spring waters were known for their health benefits. The aloe vera that grows in Gran Canaria is believed to be of the best in the world. During the 1960s, Eduardo Filiputti used the dunes at Maspalomas for heliotherapy treatments and the island's volcanic stones, seawater (rich in iodine and sodium) as well as seamud are used in a range of health therapies.

Hikers can take on Gran Canaria's own version of the Camino de Santiago pilgrimage trail. The route travels from Maspalomas in the south to Galdar in the north. It includes a visit to El Garanon and ends at San Bartolome de Tirajana, regarded as one of the island's holiest churches.

The original native Canarians were called Guanches and they were a mysterious group of people. They were tall, with blonde hair and other features unlike those of aborigines in other nearby regions such as Africa. They were not seafarers and did not use boats despite their proximity to the coastal waters. Instead their society was centered on agriculture and barley was an important crop. The three main settlements of pre-Hispanic Gran Canaria were Galdar the capital, Telde and Arguineguín. The community power structure saw the guanarteme at the top as absolute leader, with the faycan exerting influence primarily in religious matters and playing a role in economic, military and political spheres. The people of Gran Canaria worshipped Acorán and made offerings to him. Caves on the island were used as lodges, dwellings and burial sites.

Another interesting feature of pre-Hispanic culture on Gran Canaria was the use of pintaderas. These were stamps made from clay or wood which would be used to transfer the motif of a seal onto other materials. Motifs were mainly geometric and included squares, rectangles, triangles, circles and ziz-zag patterns. They were used for a variety of purposes including marking a grain silo with the owners personal emblem.

Canarian wrestling remains popular throughout the island. Once used to settle disputes, the sport is now administered by a federation that was set up in 1943 to organize regional and inter-island events.

The Guanches did not use metals nor did they have the invention of the wheel. They also did not have a written language. Perhaps all reasons why their culture disappeared just a few decades after the colonization of the Canary Islands by Spain in 1472.

According to legend, the Guanches were noble and brave and they are a source of much pride in the Canary Islands. Particularly reverred is Doramas, a warrior remembered for his brave but futile struggle against the Spanish conquest. In spite of their inferior weaponry they put up strong resistance to the invading soldiers of Spain and many Spanish soldiers perished in their battles against the Guanches.

The Pueblo Canario cultural square is often full of contemporary Canarian culture. Local dancing and singing are performed on Sunday mornings and you will also find the Museo Nestor, an art gallery dedicated to the life and works of the most famous painter from the island, Nestor Fernandez de la Torre.

Gran Canaria holds annual "fiestas" (religious festivals) and they celebrate the feast days of the patron saints in villages across the island. Statues of Jesus and the Virgin Mary are paraded throughout each village to commemorate the events. After the parade, the villagers gather to dance and drink (mostly rum and red wine) in the town squares.

The religion of 90% of Gran Canaria is Catholic as is typical of Spain. The country colonized the Canary Islands in the 15th century.

Many of those who arrived as immigrants to Gran Canaria in recent times maintain links to their native Cuba and Venezuela and the form of Spanish spoken in the Canary Islands is more akin to that spoken in Cuba than in mainland Spain.

Planning Your Stay

Gran Canaria is one of the Canary Islands and is one of Spain's autonomous regions. It is located 62 kilometers east of Tenerife and 83 kilometers west of Fuerteventura. The east coast is flat and dotted with beaches and the west coast is rocky and mountainous. Gran Canaria is located in the Atlantic Ocean, and has the same latitude as Florida in the USA. It is situated about 150 kilometers northwest of the coast of Africa and is 1,250 kilometers from Cadiz, Spain.

The capital, Las Palmas has a population of 400,000 and Gran Canaria has a population of close to 1,000,000. It is almost circular in shape and has a diameter of 45 kilometers and a surface area of 1,553 square kilometers.

Gran Canaria and the other Canary Islands are part of Macaronesia, a group of Eastern Atlantic islands that includes the Azores, Madeira, and the Cape Verdes.

Over 2 million tourists visit Gran Canaria annually with the majority of tourists staying in resorts on the southeast coast like Maspalomas and Playa del Ingles because of the preferable climate, beaches, and other amenities.

Climate & Weather

The climate of Gran Canaria is regarded as the best in Europe according to a study made by Syracuse University in the USA. Gran Canaria receives heat from the Sahara Desert and is cooled by the ocean currents from Northern Europe.

Gran Canaria receives an average of 8 hours of sunshine every day and its temperature is rarely below 20°C. Sunshine and warmth even during winter are almost guaranteed.

A majority of tourists visit the southern region of the island where the weather is warmer and imore sunny with less rain than in the north. Rainfall occurs mainly in the cooler months from October to April with the summer period between May and September being virtually rainless.

The temperature in Gran Canaria averages 17°C in winter, and 25°C in summer and is ideal for winter breaks and summer holidays. In fact, Gran Canaria and the rest of the Canarian archipelago is a great holiday destination at any time of the year. Altitude does play a role, with the higher regions generally being cooler.

Cheap flights are available from carriers like Jet2, RyanAir and EasyJet, year-round. A regular ferry service connects Las Palmas in Gran Canaria to Santa Cruz in Tenerife, Lanzarote, Puerto del Rosario in Fuerteventura, Funchal in Madeira and Cadiz on the Spanish mainland.

Sightseeing

Maspalomas

From Maspalomas to its twin resort Playa del Ingles, the beach and adjacent sand dunes stretch over a distance of 8 kilometers, covering a vast area of 250 hectares. Especially around sunset, this area offers spectacular scenery and photo opportunities.

In front of the sand dunes, the beach stretches from the lighthouse "El Faro" to the farthest end of Playa del Ingles. It is safe to swim in the sea depending on conditions but you are advised to stay close to the lifeguard towers, situated at either end of the beach.

Maspalomas Beach resembles an oasis with its palm trees and sand dunes. It is located in an idyllic setting where you can spread out your towel on the sand and enjoy a few hours of sunbathing. Sunbeds and parasols are available for rent and refreshments such as cold drinks and snacks are sold at cafe kiosks which are located every few hundred meters.

Lighthouse (El Faro)

A distinctive building on the horizon of Maspalomas is its lighthouse known as El Faro de Maspalomas. Construction began in 1861, but the project was only completed 29 years later in February 1890. At 65m, it is the third highest lighthouse in Spain. The surrounding promenade is a popular spot for people watching and for visiting some of the best bars, restaurants, cafes and ice cream parlors in Gran Canaria. You may also run into an enterprising street entertainer or two, or find a bargain at the nearby craftmarket and other shopping outlets. The lighthouse serves as an informal landmark to indicate the starting point of the Maspalomas dunes.

Botanical Park (El Parque Botanico)

Avda. del Touroperador Neckermann, 1, Urbanización Campo, Maspalomas, Gran Canaria, Spain

The botanical garden at Maspalomas is smaller than the one in Las Palmas but certainly provides a tranquil alternative to the beach and the sand dunes. It even has its own microclimate. The garden includes olives, figs, sugarcane, mango trees and cotton bushes as well as boabab trees. There are aromatic and medicinal plants and you may see butterflies and dragonflies as you stroll the walkways of the botanical garden. Admission is free.

Banana Park

Carretera Los Palmitos, Maspalomas
Tel: 928 141475

Gran Canaria has always been a banana-growing region and the fruit is still a key export crop contributing to the island's economy. Located close to Palmitos Park, Banana Park offers visitors the opportunity to take a closer look at the business of cultivating bananas. The Finca has a plantation of 4000 bananas and also grows aloe vera, papaya, tomatoes and oranges. There are various animals on the property including apes, camels, donkeys, goats, cows, black canarian pigs and there is an aviary and a special butterfly house. Fruit juice and other local products can be bought from the souvenir shop at reasonable prices. Admission is €7.

Holiday World

Avda. Touroperador Tui, 35100 Maspalomas, Gran Canaria, Spain
Tel: 928 73 04 98

Holiday World at Maspalomas provides a selection of amusements for all ages. There are indoor and outdoor activities. A variety of rides include a pirate ship, a rodeo ride and a cat and mouse rollercoaster. There are trampolines, bouncing castles and shooting stalls, as well as a park that offers a boating lake, a kart track and pony rides. A popular attraction is the 27 meter Ferriss Wheel, which also enables spectacular views of the nearby mountain. For the health conscious, there is a wellness center that provides spa treatments and access to a well-equipped gym. Adults can enjoy a host of nighttime entertainment such as karaoke sessions and the vibrant fun of a salsa club. Entrance is free, with rides being charged separately, but there is the option of an unlimited rider ticket for €30. Holiday World offers free parking and free Wi-Fi.

Aqualand

Aqualand is located near Maspalomas in the southern part of Gran Canaria on the road to Palmitos Park. Because of the favorable weather conditions on the island, the park is open all year round. It is the biggest water park in Gran Canaria, with an area of 90,000 square meters. The park's pools alone cover 5,300 square meters. It is ideal for an outing with your young children. There are 33 slides and 13 other attractions which include Tornado, Surf Beach, Congo River, Crazy Race, Kamikaze, Rapids, Aquamania, Twister and many others. Tornado is the main attraction of the park, featuring a huge slide with a series of exciting turns and large slopes.

Onsite are self-service restaurants as well as a pizzeria, coffee shops, bars, and other facilities.

You can reach Aqualand by car or by taking a bus from Playa del Ingles, Bahia Feliz, Puerto Rico or Faro, Maspalomas.

Palmitos Park

Palmitos Park is located 10 kilometers north of the beach and the sand dunes of Maspalomas and Playa del Ingles. It covers an area of 20 hectares and has been developed as a botanical garden and aviary.

The park features thousands of palm trees, a variety of orchids and many exotic creatures. Birds of prey and other exotic birds in the park include falcons, parrots, and eagles. You will also see many swans and ducks. There are a range of cacti and other succulents in excellent condition. The park has over 160 cactus types and 1000 palm trees of 42 types.

Palmitos Park is located in a mountainous park and provides visitors with a chance to see beautiful landscapes as they walk around the park. A small terrace leads to an amphitheater, where trained birds of prey perform in shows for visitors. Beside the amphitheater is a snack bar and a cafeteria can also be found in the park.

Playa del Ingles

Playa del Ingles (meaning "beach of the English") is the biggest and liveliest resort in Gran Canaria. It lies between the smaller but more upscale resorts, Maspalomas and San Agustin. Together they share a beach that is 8 kilometers long. From the airport, Playa del Ingles can be reached in 30 minutes by car or bus via the main highway.

Playa del Ingles is a popular beach for the young (particularly the 18-30 age group) who flock to the island during the summer months of July and August. During the rest of the year it also attracts tourists of all ages.

There are few historical monuments or cultural sights of note in the resort. Instead the focus is on bars, cafes, high-rise hotels, shopping malls, and fast-food restaurants. Established in 1960, the resort has become famous throughout Europe. Two of the biggest shopping centers in Playa del Ingles are Yumbo Centrum at Avenida de Espana and Kasbah at Plaza Telde.

Spend the day in Playa del Ingles on the beach or take part in various watersports such as jet skiing, diving and paragliding or stroll along the promenade Paseo Costa Canaria while you take in the tropical flora and luxurious villas. At night the scenery changes dramatically as discos and nightclubs spin into action until the small hours.

If you want to attend church during your holiday at Playa del Ingles, Templo Ecumenico de San Salvador offers ecumenical, interdenominational services in three languages. Its decorative wrought iron gates and beautiful stained glass windows are impressive and the architecture is modern and eclectic.

Nightlife

With year round sunny weather and a fairly close proximity to Europe and the United Kingdom, Gran Canaria attracts a lively crowd of holidaymakers, particularly in the 18 to 30 years age group. This has resulted in a vibrant nightclub scene with a variety entertainment options available. The night usually begins late, with many bars staying open until 2am and most clubs still partying at 6am.

The liveliest area on the island is Playa del Ingles. One of the biggest clubs is Pacha, in the Kasbah Center, which was established in 1984. This disco-pub offers good decor, great music and a wonderful ambiance. Club Ozono plays a selection of music including electronic, techno, R&B, house and hip-hop. Located within Hotel Buenaventura, this popular venue also hosts events such as the MTV music awards. Chic & Cream in Hotel Maritim Playa plays house music, as spun by some of the top international DJs. Another location where you can expect the best DJs from around the world is Costa Chinawhite. It is in the Kasbah Center and the music is mainly hip-hop and R&B. An equally trendy nightspot in Maspalomas is Bachira, where you can party the night away with a host of Go-Go dancers.

British visitors may recognize Highlanders in Puerto Rico as a home away from home. This Scottish pub offers various British choices and will prove particularly popular with sport lovers. Nowanda Cafe in Las Palmas is a haven for jazz lovers. For free live music, consider paying a visit to Cuasquias, on Calle San Pedro in Las Palmas. If you fancy a date with Lady Luck, there are two casinos on Gran Canaria. Casino Las Palmas is located in Hotel Santa Catalina, whereas Gran Canaria Casino is in Hotel Melia Tamarindos in San Augustin. The Wigwam Cocktail Bar in Puerto Rico has a Native American theme.

The Playa del Ingles region is also a popular destination for gay visitors with the Yumbo Center acting as an epicenter for parties and other activities. These range from relaxing watering holes to raunchy cruise bars with a men-only policy and dress-down code. One of the most popular clubs is Heaven, which plays mostly house music and hosts lively parties. Drag shows are performed at Ricky's Caberet Bar, Cafe La Belle and Sparkles Show Bar, which also hosts karaoke. There are several German-owned establishments such as the Wunderbar, Adonis, Rainbow Bistro Cafe, Na Und, Gio and Macho Macho, a Danish gay bar called Meicker, the English gay bar, Diamonds and Jackie's Bar, which attracts a female crowd.

Las Palmas

Las Palmas is the capital of Gran Canaria and is situated in the northeast of the island. With a population of about 400,000, it is the biggest city on the island and is 20 kilometers from Las Palmas International Airport.

Two of the best attractions for tourists to Las Palmas are its two sandy beaches, La Playa de las Canteras and Playa de las Alcaravaneras. Playa de las Alcaravaneras is located by the Muelle Deportivo marina and has one kilometer of golden sand. The beach is used as a base for aquatic sports such as sailing.

Near the Playa de las Alcaravaneras is the Parque Doramas. This park is home to many of the islands "autochthonous" plants (local native plants) such as dragon trees. The park was designed by the architect Miguel Martin Fernandez de la Torre in 1922. Within the park are three significant buildings. The Pueblo Canario Museum displays traditional Canarian architecture. Museo Nestor is a museum dedicated to Nestor Martin Fernandez de la Torre, who was an important painter and a symbolist, and one of two famous brothers that left their mark on Gran Canaria. The park also includes the historical Hotel Santa Catalina which was built in the colonial style in 1890.

Pueblo Canario Museum is a complex featuring island houses built along traditional lines and is laid out to form a typical Canarian village. The museum was the brainchild of Nestor Martin Fernandez de la Torre and construction was by his architect brother, Miguel. Pueblo Canario is considered to be the highlight of their careers and both brothers are a source of national pride to the people of Gran Canaria. Its large open-air central square serves as a stage for performances showing local folklore of Gran Canaria.

Puerto de la Luz, located near Playa de las Alcaravaneras, is one of the most important ports in Spain. Visit to watch the popular sport of Vela Latina (Canarian sailing) with regattas taking place almost every weekend.

A popular event held in Las Palmas during the first quarter of the year is its carnival (see later.)

Las Palmas also holds the festival of the Fundacionales de San Juan (Saint John Festival) to commemorate the founding of the city, an event that is held on the feast day of St. John the Baptist, as it is called in other Catholic countries.

Las Palmas has four large shopping centers: Las Arenas (the biggest on the island), La Ballena, 7 Palmas and El Muelle (probably the best.)

You can also shop for traditional products in four markets: Vegueta, el Puerto, Alcaravaneras and Alta Vista. You will find craft fairs on Sundays in both Pueblo Canario and Vegueta. The FEDAC shop in Triana is the official outlet for craftwork and an antique market is held on the first Sunday of each month in Santa Catalina Park.

Playa de las Canteras

Playa de las Canteras Beach is one of four major beaches in Gran Canaria, and it is the most popular. The impressive promenade Paseo de Canteras runs parallel to the beach. The presence of street entertainers, artists and street vendors are added attractions. Playa de las Canteras was the first tourist resort of Gran Canaria, and is bordered on the east by Santa Catalina and to the north by La Isleta.

The beach has a natural barrier reef known as "La Barra", which breaks the waves as they come into the beach. The reef is about 200 meters long and is responsible for creating a natural lagoon. The beach is ideal for a number of water sports and it is a great spot for surfing.

At Playa de las Canteras you will find the biggest shopping center in Gran Canaria, Las Arenas, which is situated in front of Alfredo Kraus Auditorium at the northwest corner of the beach. (Alfredo Kraus was a famous tenor singer from Gran Canaria.)

Vegueta

The name "Vegueta" comes from the Spanish word "vega" which refers to a fertile plain. It is the oldest town of Las Palmas and because of its historical and cultural significance, Vegueta has been declared a World Heritage site by UNESCO.

GRAN CANARIA TRAVEL GUIDE

At Plaza Santa Ana in Vegueta, you will notice bronze statues of dogs. They symbolize the appearance of dogs in Las Palmas in the early 16th century. Gran Canaria is known as "The Island of Dogs".

The most important historical buildings in Las Palmas can be found in Vegueta and some of the buildings have stood for more than 500 years, including the Chapel of San Antonio Abad, Plaza Santa Ana, Obispado, and Casa Regental. It is said that the chapel is where Christopher Columbus visited to pray during his journey to discover the Americas.

The Santa Ana Cathedral on Plaza Santa Ana has been superbly preserved over the centuries. The Casa de Colon (Christopher Columbus museum) records the voyages to America of this famous explorer. Vegueta also includes the Museo Canario which contains relics of the Guanches (the native inhabitants of the island.) Another museum, The Museum of Sacred Art, displays religious works. The area also has an impressive old market that dates back to the 19th century.

Casa de Colon

Calle Colon 1, 35001, Las Palmas
Tel: 928 312 373

Casa de Colon is located in the southeastern sector of Las Palmas in Vegueta. The area is more than 500 years old and is known for its cobbled streets and historical charm. The building has a number of impressive features, including an attractive facade, ornate doorways, spacious courtyards and intricately latticed balconies. The building served as a residence for the early governors of the island and it was rebuilt in 1777. Today's house resulted from the integration of several buildings and it now occupies an entire block.

Casa de Colon is named after its most famous guest, Christopher Columbus. During his epic journey of discovery to the New World, Christopher Columbus stayed here while repairs were made to his ship, La Pinta. Various exhibits are focused on this event including nautical maps, charts, paintings and navigational instruments. There are also many personal notes and first impressions of the Americas. Most impressive is an authentic replica of a ship's cabin, based on the actual cabin of the ship, La Niña.

There are thirteen permanent exhibition halls and other displays are dedicated to the history of the Canary Islands, the relation between the American colonies and the Canaries, and the changing face of Las Palmas, as illustrated through a series of models. Admission is free.

Triana

Triana is located near to Vegueta, and is located on one side of Guiniguada ravine. Here, you can enjoy a pleasant walk along the Calle Mayor de Triana, admiring buildings of great artistic and historical value. San Telmo Park in Triana includes the chapel of San Telmo, a modern pavilion and a bandstand. The park features mature landscaping with large palm trees and is where visitors should go to experience some peace in this often busy city. Nearby the Teatro Perez Galdos is a theater of Italian design, is one of the most noteworthy buildings in Las Palmas.

Other architectural structures in the area surrounding Triana include the Edificio Quegles which was built in 1900 and the Casa Museo Perez Galdos, which contains an archive of Benito Perez Galdos, who was born in the house. Galdos was a famous Spanish author who lived between 1843 and 1920. The building represents a fine example of 18th century Canarian architecture and some of the exhibits include drawings and paintings by Galdos as well as mementos from his career and first proofs of his work. Admission is €3.

Teror
Teror is one of the oldest and most beautiful towns in Gran Canaria. When you visit your attention will be drawn to the famous Basilica of the La Senora de Pino (Virgin of the Pine) as well as to the distinctive architectural style of the buildings.

The Basilica is a magnificent landmark dedicated to the Virgin Mary, who, some inhabitants of Gran Canaria say, appeared here on September 8, 1481. The town celebrates the Feast of the Virgin of the Pine on this same date every year. The festival begins with a parade featuring the centuries-old statue of the Blessed Virgin, and ends with a late night, open-air celebration, common to parties on the island.

Plaza del Pino is a vast plaza in the center of Teror and is surrounded by elegant homes. These homes are built in the characteristic colonial style with doors, windows, and balconies made of dark carved wood. Many of these structures date back to the 1500s, and because of their unique architectural features, the center of the town of Teror was declared a national monument.

The Sunday market in Teror offers you a wide range of goods, including some of its specialties, like the spicy sausage Chorizo de Teror, sweets made by nuns in the locality, and handicrafts of various kinds.

During your visit you can also have a taste of Teror's famous mineral water, Agua de Teror, which comes from a natural spring just outside the town.

Cenobia de Valeron (Valeron Monastery)

Las Palmas, Gran Canaria

Located on the north coast, the enigmatic honeycomb of caves has fascinated visitors for centuries. The entrance to the site is an arch of red-yellow basalt, some 20 meters high and 28 meters wide and once inside, you will find a collection of some 300 caves and other cavities. These were hand-carved using flint tools, by the island's prehistoric population. Various uses have been ascribed to the caves. They are sometimes referred to as Valeron Monastery, a moniker that alludes to the allegation that the caves were once the site of a convent or monastery. It has also been suggested that the site may have been used to prepare girls for marriage.

Its most likely function was for a fortified granary, since similar facilities, known as "agadirs" have been found in other locations around North Africa. Some of the foods that might have been stored here could have included barley, figs and salted meat. Once filled, a wooden plank would have covered the cavities, or silos, with a pintado or seal being used to mark it. The higher the cave, the more suited it was to the preservation of the stored food. The person in charge was most likely a "faican" or leader who had jurisdiction over religious, political and economical matters.

The site was visited by the 18th century historian Pedro Agustin, as well as the anthopologist Rene Verneau, who complained about the damage caused by looters. Today, the site is easily accessible and well signposted, with displays providing information on the site itself, as well as animals and plantlife of the surrounding areas. It offers great views, as well as insight into the indigenous people of Gran Canaria before the arrival of the Spanish. Admission is €2.50.

Mundo Aborigen (Aborigine World)

Carretera Fataga, Km 6, 35108 Fataga, Las Palmas

If you wish to gain an insight into life in Gran Canaria before the arrival of the Spanish, Mundo Aborigen provides a fascinating glimpse. Overlooking the gorge of Barranco de Fataga, the theme park consists of a reconstructed Canaria village, set on 100,000 square meters. There are over 100 life-sized figures arranged to depict a variety of typical activities. Scenes show aspects of life, ranging from agricultural chores, household chores and a doctor at work, to a prisoner getting capital punishment meted out and two youths wrestling. An audio sound track features realistic animal noises and actors are employed to demonstrate specific elements and activities. For further realism, this open-air museum also has live animals on the property. There is a clearly marked trail, with informative displays in Spanish, English and German.

Caldera de Bandama

Santa Brigida, 35300 Las Palmas de Gran Canaria, Gran Canaria, Spain

The Caldera de Bandama is located between three of the island's municipalities, namely Las Palmas de Gran Canaria, Santa Brigida and Telde and bears testimony to the powerful volcanic eruptions that caused the creation of Gran Canaria. The crater is almost 1 kilometer wide and 200 meters deep. The highest point of the rim is Pico de Bandama, where it reaches 569 meters. Expect the descent to take approximately an hour. At the bottom of the crater, you will be able to observe the various different hues of ashes, as well as a number of interesting plant species, such as the very rare Dama de Bandama flower. There are also lots of bird species and a fair amount of lizards.

It is possible to book <u>an organized hike</u> to the bottom of the crater, often with a picnic lunch included. The area enables stunning panoramic views of the surroundiing landscape. The fertile soil near the volcano is utilized for vineyards and visitors can combine a volcano tour with a winery visit.

Gran Canaria Carnival

The carnival in Gran Canaria is the modern representation of an ancient tradition which originated in the 16th century. The word "carnival" comes from the expression, "carnem levare" meaning "remove the meat" or "farewell to the flesh."

But what a farewell party! Carnival's wild partying and festivities immediately precede the Lent season which starts on Ash Wednesday (traditionally a day of fasting).

Through the years Carnival has evolved and includes processions of floats, fireworks, bizarre masks, colorful costumes, dancers (known as "murgas" and "comparsas"), singers, merrymakers and loud Latin music. There is a contest to select the Carnival queen as well as the best band, dancers, singers and other entertainers. The contest is held in the weeks prior to the Carnival and the winners are announced at the start of the festivities. Carnival is taken very seriously in Gran Canaria and it often takes the whole year to design and make the costume of the Carnival queen.

Carnival is celebrated by parades in many towns across the island on different days. The best parades are in Las Palmas, Playa del Ingles, Arguineguin, Agaete, and Telde where the revelry begins at dusk and ends at dawn. Carnival starts in late-February, and ends on Ash Wednesday, the start of the Lent season which is observed by traditional Catholics as a period of fasting and abstinence.

Carnival is one of the very best times to visit Gran Canaria. So pack (or buy locally) a costume and mask and join in with the fun in one of the processions on the island.

Arucas

Arucas marks an important battlefield in the conquest of Gran Canaria. Originally known as Arehucas, it was here that the Spanish invaders clashed with local warriors led by the courageous Doramas. The Canarii leader initially challenged the Spanish to single combat between himself and one of their champions. The duel was won by Doramas who was mortally wounded by Pedro de Vera. As a result, the Spanish took the town. Montana de Arucas is believed to mark the spot where Doramas was killed.

Arucas is located in mountainous terrain in the north and is surrounded by farmland including sugarcane plantations. The town has a large rum distillery, a striking neo-Gothic church, attractive plazas, historical buildings in the Old Town and a botanical garden. A product of the region is cochinilla, a red dye made from the crushed shells of the beetle of the same name. Arucas is today considered almost a suburb of Las Palmas and has a population of 33,000. It is accessible by car or bus from San Telmo in Las Palmas.

Iglesia de San Juan Bautista

Calle Parroco Morales, 35400 Arucas, Gran Canaria
Tel: 34-928-600092

Located at the heart of the suburb, Arucas, the church of Saint John the Baptist or Iglesia de San Juan Bautista is a commanding sight. The opulent Gothic style resembles that of a cathedral, and the church has various noteworthy features. The congregation it represents, dates back to 1515, but the present building is of more recent construction. Designed by the architect, Manuel Vega March, work began in 1909. Local stone was employed, as well as local artisans and the interior includes several paintings by Christobal Hernandez de Quintana, a Reclining Christ carved by Manuel Ramos and some beautiful stained glass work. Admission is free. The attractive little square in front of the church is a popular place to indulge in a little people watching or just soak up the atmosphere.

Arehucas Rum Distillery

Apartado de Correos 1, 35400 Arucas, Gran Canaria, Spain
Tel: (34) 928 624 900

Arucas has been an important sugar cane growing area since the 15th century and the town is home to the largest rum distillery in the Canary Islands. Here, you will be able to take a closer look at various aspects of the rum industry, through a series of informative displays and exhibits. A tour of the facility will enable you to view the bottling plant or compare just how much bottle designs have evolved, through a collection of containers from different periods. Look for the barrels which have been autographed by politicians and celebrities. The tour ends with a tasting session, that will enable you to sample some of the distillery's more unique creations such as honey rum, chocolate rum and banana flavored rum. There is a small gift shop where you can buy rum and a variety of related products. The rum distillery dates back to 1884. Admission is free.

Sioux City, Bahia Feliz

Sioux City is a make-believe western town located in Canon del Aguila (Canyon of the Eagle) near Bahia Feliz. It covers a massive area of 320,000 square meters. The site was built as the set for the film "Take a Hard Ride." On a visit, you see two daily shows featuring cowboys and Indians depicting the days of the "Wild West" in the USA. Sioux City features cattle stampedes, gunfights, and Indian tepees. Some of the events staged for your entertainment include a Bank Robbery, Saloon Fight, Town Square Hanging, Indian Rain Dance, and other scenes from westerns and other movies.

You can dine in Sioux City's Three Stars Saloon or the BBQ Station where you can pretend that you are in a 19th century western town. You might even bump into one of your Western heroes but don't be disappointed if one of them is not really Clint Eastwood or John Wayne!

La Cumbre

La Cumbre (The Summit) is located at the center of Gran Canaria. It is a rugged mountainous region with charming villages. It has winding roads, which you can use for a rigorous trek up the mountains or, if you are not up to this kind of activity, you can choose to take a more leisurely hike along gentler roads that lead to the miradores or viewing areas. Here, you can enjoy a breathtaking view of the surrounding landscape.

Pico de las Nieves (Snow Peak), and Roque Nublo (Cloudy Rock/Misty Rock), are two of the best places to begin your sightseeing in La Cumbre. Pico de Las Nieves rises 1,950 meters high, and it is the highest point in Gran Canaria. Roque Nublo is an 80-meter monolith, and has become the emblem of Gran Canaria.

Roque Nublo is 1,813 meters high, more than 100 meters lower than Pico de las Nieves and you can get to its summit by hiking for about 30 minutes. During your hike look for the miradores from which you can enjoy breathtaking views of the southern part of Gran Canaria including Maspalomas, Playa del Ingles, and Puerto Mogan. At the summit, you will be able to see the famous monolith and the snow-capped Mount Teide on the island of Tenerife.

At Roque Nublo, you can view three interesting rock formations: El Fraile (The Monk), La Rana (The Frog), and Roque Bentayga. These were pre-Hispanic places of worship with caves hewn out of vertical cliffs.

The next item in your itinerary should be a visit to one of the highland towns such as Tejeda. The town is a sight to behold especially in February or March, when the winter rains make the almond trees blossom. Another nearby town is Artenara, the smallest of the municipalities in the highlands. It is an intriguing place, where you can stop by homes and hotels constructed in caves. The main attraction of Artenara is the cave church, the Santuario de la Virgen Cuevita.

Telde

The town of Telde is located on a plain in one of the most fertile parts of Gran Canaria on the northeastern side of the island. The surrounding land is used to grow sugar cane, bananas, cucumber and flowers. With a population of over 80,000, it is the second largest town on Gran Canaria, located about 13km south of Las Palmas beside the province's main highway.

Along with Galdar, Telde had been one of the pre-Hispanic kingdoms of Gran Canaria. The aboriginal warrior, Doramas is believed to have lived in Telde. La Montana de las Cuatro Puertas is a site located at the south of the city on the way to Ingenio. It was considered holy by the indigenous Guanche population. The hilltop complex features a large chamber with four entrances. It was used for ancient burials of the rich and famous.

Telde's charming historical center is Plaza de San Juan, an attractive square flanked by trees and colonial buildings. The most impressive of these is the Basilica de San Juan Bautista. Inside the church, you will find the rather unusual Christ of Telde, a 1.85m statue made of corncobs. It is the work of the Michoacan Indians of Mexico. Equally striking is the Flemish altarpiece, which depicts six scenes from the life of the Virgin Mary.

Ingenio

Located between the ravines of Barranco de Aguatona and Barranco de Guayadeque, Ingenio is one of the oldest towns in Gran Canaria. The town grew prosperous during the 16th century when it was known for its sugar refining capabilities. Equipment remnants can be seen in a disused sugar cane pressing machine on the eastern side of town. Nowadays tomatoes are regarded as the most important crop.

Central to the town is the Plaza de la Candelaria with its contemporary fountains and Town Hall. Its most promenent building is the Iglesia de Nuestra Senora de la Candelaria, a colonial style church which dates back to 1901 which is dedicated to the patron saint of the Canaries. The building has two towers and a prominent white dome and was built on the foundations of a previous chapel. The church bells are of Cuban origin and the main altarpiece is Gothic.

The Clock House (Casa del Reloj) is in the center. It is the property of the Royal Water Rights Association of Aguatona, an organisation that represents the water irrigation rights of farmers. Also of interest is the Water Mills Route (Ruta de los Molinos de Agua) which demonstrates the working of the water mills in the historical quarter. Parque Nestor offers a tranquil spot of rest and relaxation. There are two beaches, of which the more popular is Playa del Burrero, a beach that offers great conditions for sailing and windsurfing.

Another attraction in Ingenio is the Stone and Craft Museum (Museo de Piedra y Artesania). Its collection includes pottery, wickerwork and agricultural tools, as well as rocks and mineral specimens. The museum has a gift shop where you can buy pottery, lace and palm-woven products. The town hosts an International Folklore Festival that includes participants from Mexico, Russia and Uganda. The area is also known for the quality of its embroidery and lace work and has an embroidery school.

Nearby is the prehistoric site called Barranco de Guayadeque. It is a ravine that features many natural, manmade caves that have served as dwellings or burial places. Various hiking trails link to the different caves and the Guayadeque Museum demonstrates what the area must have looked like when inhabited by the indigenous people.

Puerto Mogan

The Puerto Mogan marina is located on the southwest coast of Gran Canaria. It is a picturesque resort and marina that is about 40-minutes drive by car from the airport. The resort offers water sports like parasailing, jet skiing, scuba diving and even a submarine tour. If you prefer less strenuous activities, you can watch dolphins or take a boat ride.

The resort is dubbed, "La Venecia de Canarias" (Venice of the Canaries) because of the canals between the marina and the harbor which pass under arches in buildings and between the port and the beach. The harbor is one of the most popular ports in the Canary Islands.

Residential buildings in Puerto Mogan are built in the Mediterranean style and do not exceed three storeys. They are built along narrow alleys that are resplendid with flowers, mostly bougainvilleas.

Aloe Vera Museum

Calle Rivera del Carmen no 5, 35139 Puerto de Mogan, Gran Canaria, Spain

Aloe Vera is a succulent shrub that occurs naturally in North Africa and in the Canary Islands. Knowledge of its therapeutic value dates back to the time of ancient Egypt, where both Cleopatra and Queen Nefertiti used it for skincare. Christopher Columbus regarded it as essential for healing.

The shrub can benefit a variety of ailments, including constipation, ulcers and inflammation and it is also known to repair the damage of UV radiation. Aloe is rich in minerals and can aid weight loss.

Some of the finest quality aloe vera grows on Gran Canaria. To learn more about the story of aloe vera and its uses, pay a visit to the Aloe Vera Museum, or Information Center, which is located in the town of Puerto de Mogan.

Puerto Rico

Puerto Rico is one of the sunniest locations in Gran Canaria making it an ideal setting for a resort. It has plenty of shops, restaurants, a pleasant sandy beach and is flanked by an expansive port development. The town is popular for sailing and as a base for big game fishing excursions. It offers an abundance of blue marlin, white marlin, tuna and swordfish in nearby waters. There are facilities for water sports including jetskiing, diving and windsurfing. Other popular activities include dolphin watching and glass-bottom boat trips that provide an intriguing glimpse below the surface of the sea. To be pampered you can visit the Gloria Palace Amadores Spa for a relaxing hydromassage in their saltwater jacuzzi.

Angry Birds Theme Park

Puerto Rico, Gran Canaria

Angry Birds, the popular mobile game created by the Finnish game designer Jaakko Iisalo, was first released in December 2009 and went on to become a phenomenal success, inspiring various related events and merchandise. The first Angry Birds theme park opened in Finland in 2012, paving the way for several similar establishments to be set up, including one of the most recent, a theme park in Gran Canaria, which opened in October 2013.

GRAN CANARIA TRAVEL GUIDE

Following the themes of various versions of the game, the facility includes a Classic and Space section. It features attractions such as the Air Somersault Track, a Bag Jump a Pedal Car Track, a Lazer Room, a Learning Room, an Arcade Room and Terence's Wheel. A separate part of the park is dedicated to an Adventure Golf course and there is also a gift shop and a snack room. The Angry Birds theme park is located on Gran Canaria's main strip, near the bus station. Admission is €15.

Galdar

Galdar is located on the northwestern coast of Gran Canaria. The town begins at the base of a volcano, with some of its residential properties spread towards the higher slopes. It is surrounded by many banana plantations. Once the capital of a pre-Hispanic Gran Canaria, it now has a population of around 25,000. The town has a charming colonial square flanked by a neo-Classical style church, Santiago de Galdar. Another feature is the Drago or dragon tree, which dates back to 1718.

There are several tidal pools nearby, notably at El Agujero, Dos Roques, La Caleta de Arriba, La caleta de Abajo and La Rada del Juncal. Bear in mind that these pools only offer safe swimming conditions during low tide. Also near Galdar, is the La Guancha cemetery, which dates back to the 11th century and includes the remains of various members of Gran Canaria's Guanche aristocracy. There are great locations nearby for mountain-biking, as well as hiking, such as the Tamadaba pine forest.

Another attraction near Galdar is Parque Norte on the road to Sardina del Norte. Here you can find a diverse collection of palm trees and banana plantations, as well as a selection of exotic animals including marmosets, toucans, Japanese flamingo and parrots. There is also a petting zoo with dwarf pigs and donkeys, rabbits, goats and turtles and various interesting pathways. Admission is €12.

Painted Cave (La Cueva Pintada de Gáldar)

Audiencia, 2, 35460 Galdar, Gran Canaria, Spain
Tel: 928 89 54 89

The Painted Cave at Galdar (La Cueva Pintada de Gáldar) is regarded as one of the most important archaeological finds in the Canary Islands. Discovered in 1873 by the farmer José Ramos Orihuela, the site features an intriguing collection of geometric motifs, painted in white and red pigment.

Today, the complex includes a museum, a heritage center and, of course, the excavated area itself. Access is provided through a network of elevated walkways. A 3D film explores various indigenous myths and folklore. The cave itself can be viewed by the public, but from a transparent perspex chamber, to protect the original cave art. It re-opened in 2006, after being closed for restoration work. The site can only be visited via guided tours. Admission is €6.

Surfing

Surfing is a popular activity with the locals. The best waves occur between September and April and the period between November and February is the peak season when there are consistent swells of between 1.8 and 2.4 meters.

A premier surf spot on Gran Canaria is El Confital, which is within walking distance of La Puntilla. The wave action is powerful, fast and recommended for experienced surfers. It is considered one of the best right-hand reef breaks in the Canary Islands and swells of up to 3 meters can be experienced. This beach can get super crowded, especially over weekends.

The beach of Pozo Izquierdo at the town of St Lucia offers ideal conditions for windsurfing. There is a windsurfing center and an international championship is hosted here. Other locations ideal for windsurfing include Galdar in the northeast and Playa de Las Canteras in Las Palmas. Playa de Vargas is one of the venues used for the PWA Wave Classic Grand Prix. Windspeeds here can reach up to 60 kilometers per hour.

Along the northeastern coast of Gran Canaria, conditions are also suitable for kitesurfing, with some of the best locations being Bahía Feliz, Vargas and Las Canteras.

Crocodile Park

Carretera Gral Los Coralillos, Aguimes

The Crocodile Park can be described as an animal sanctuary, rather than a zoo. It was first opened to the public in 1988. Founded when the Balser family took in the first adoptees, the facility now has over 300 crocodiles, making it home to the largest collection of crocodiles in Europe. Most of the animals are rescues, often from the illegal trade in exotic pets, or donations. There is, however, a large variety of different crocodile species, as well as different types of parrots, primates like chimpanzees, several species of small monkeys, terrapins, a large tortoise and even a tiger. Additionally, the park also has a variety of domestic animals such as pygmy goats, horses, pigs, guinea pigs and rabbits.

There are two daily shows, a parrot show at noon and, the highlight of the day, a crocodile show and public feeding, which lasts about 30 minutes, at 1pm. Visitors will also be able to handle small crocodiles and at the canteen, you can buy a bunch of bananas to feed various of the animals, for only €1. Admission is €10 and a free bus service is available.

Camel Park, Arteara

Barranco Arteara, San Bartolome de Tirajana
Tel: +34 670 674 029

The Spanish from Castile first brought camels to the Canaries with their conquest more than 600 years ago. At the Camel Park, you can enjoy the bumpy treat of a camel ride along a scenic route through the palm groves. Part of the tour includes a trip past the pretty village of Fataga and an exploration of the enigmatic valley of Arteara, where the greenery of the northern parts give way to the landscape of the arid south. Arteara Valley includes the archaeological site of a 2500 year old necropolis. You will also be able to feed and interact with baby camels. A lunch completes the experience. The park is home to a number of other animals including sheep, pigs, donkeys, parrots and a pony.

Diving in Gran Canaria

http://www.canary-diving.com/

The Arinaga Marine Reserve, also known as El Cabron, is one of three marine reserves to be found in the Canary Islands. Due to a ban on fishing in this region, there is an abundance of diverse marine life including moray eels, dusky and silver grouper, parrotfish, triggerfish, lizardfish, rainbow wrasse, barracuda, common and electric rays as well as turtles. The site offers at least eight different dives, the deepest reaching a maximum of 30 meters. At 12 meters, El Cabron is a great site for newer divers. Other dives include the Arch and the Gorgonian. The Arinaga Marine Reserve is accessible via a dirt road.

More experienced divers may wish to challenge themselves by exploring a few of the ships wrecked around Las Palmas harbor. These range from historical vessels to more recent casualties like the Calais and the Arona. Dives can go as deep as 40 meters, but will usually be dependent on weather conditions. There is also a Russian ferry, near El Pajar, which was wrecked in 2003, and has since become the home of communities of common stingray, butterfly ray and angel shark.

The Pasito Blanco Reef has a variety of interesting rock features and ledges that house a multitude of fish. Regular marine visitors include moray eel, angel sharks and barracudas. There is likewise an abundance of soft coral to be observed.

There are plenty of opportunities for diving in the vicinity of Puerto de Mogan. These include the Taurito Reef and Taurito caves, as well as shipwrecks like the Cermona, which is inhabited by parrotfish, cornetfish, morays and various species of molluscs and crustaceans. Another wreck, the Araganza, is home to a vast community of species, including trumpet fish, moray eels and Canarian lobster. The Taurito caves were formed from volcanic action many years ago and now houses a variety of marine species. Puerto de Mogan does offer a more leisurely alternative to diving, if you wish to explore the bottom of the sea, namely its famous Yellow Submarine underwater tours.

Cactualdea (Cactus Park)

Carretera del Hoyo, Tocodomán
Tel: +34 928 891 228

Located in the western part of Gran Canaria, Cactus Park has a collection of around 1200 species of cactus, some originating from places as diverse as Mexico, Guatamala and Madagascar. These are offset against occasional palms, dragon trees and aloes. The park also has a number of animal residents, which include ostriches, goats and peacocks, as well as a Guanche cave. The restaurant serves authentic Canarian food, as well as international dishes. Another interesting feature is the amphitheatre, which is sometimes utilized for la lucha Canaria, or Canarian wrestling, a sport that is considered similar to sumo wrestling. The park has a wine cellar with over 250 different wines and tasting tours can be arranged. Admission to the park is €6.

Museo del Castillo de la Fortaleza

Tomas Arroyo Cardoso, s/n, Santa Lucia, Gran Canaria, Spain

The Museo del Castillo de la Fortaleza has an interesting collection of archaeological artefacts, most of them items of some cultural significance. These include pottery, wicker work and tools used for agricultural tasks, as well as bones and pressed flowers. There is a military display, an art gallery and a botanical garden which focusses mainly on indigenous specimens and demonstrates which ones are endemic to which altitudes.

Although the facade of the building is modern, it includes interesting features such as turrets. It is located in the town of St Lucia, near Fortress Ansite, a volcanic site with an intriguing network of aboriginal cave dwellings and burial rooms. For a look at modern versions of traditional crafts such as pottery and basketware, pay a visit to the town's craft center, where locally made items are exhibited and sold.

GRAN CANARIA TRAVEL GUIDE

Places to Stay

Cordial Mogan Valle, Puerto Mogan

Avda los Marrero 4
35138 Puerto de Mogan
Gran Canaria, Spain
Tel: +34 928143393
www.cordialcanarias.com/en/index.html
Rate: $72+/ €53+

The hotel is situated in the middle of a 35,000-square meter garden in Puerto Mogan, which is known as the "Little Venice" of Gran Canaria. It is just a few meters away from the beach, the marina, and the fishing quay. The hotel consists of apartments with one or two bedrooms. Each apartment is furnished with a microwave oven, coffee maker, fridge, satellite TV, direct dial telephone, and a private bathroom with shower. There are three swimming pools for adults and a children's pool. Wi-Fi is available in the whole hotel area.

AC Hotel Gran Canaria Marriott

Las Palmas 35007 Eduardo Benot, 3-5
Las Palmas de Gran Canaria, Spain
Tel: +34-928-266-100
http://www.marriott.com/hotels/travel/lpagr-ac-hotel-gran-canaria/
From $80+/ €59+

AC Hotel Gran Canaria by Marriott is located in the center of the city, about 300 meters from the famous Las Canteras Beach. You can walk to Sta. Catalina Park and the Museo Elder de la Ciencia from the hotel. The main shopping area is just a 10-minute stroll away. The hotel is easily accessible from the airport, which is around 20 kilometers away. Each room is air-conditioned and is equipped with cable TV, broad band Internet access for a surcharge, free mini bar that is replenished daily, a private bathroom and a big, comfortable bed. It has a rooftop swimming pool where you can view the whole city, the ocean, and the surrounding mountains.

Club Hotel Riu Gran Canaria

Las Meloneras, 35100 Maspalomas
Gran Canaria, Spain
Tel: +34-928-563-000
From $64+/ €47+

Located at the seafront on Costa Meloneras, this hotel is built amidst a 30,000-square meter garden. It is around 900 meters from Maspalomas Beach and the Sand Dunes, 200 meters from various shops, and 100 meters from a bus stop. From the hotel you can explore nearby sites like Playa de los Burras, Mogan Harbor, and the historical town of Aguimes. All rooms are air-conditioned and equipped with modern facilities, such as mini fridge, satellite TV, private bathroom, and telephone. Wireless internet is available at the lobby for a surcharge. It has 3 swimming pools for adults, a swimming pool for children, and 2 whirlpools.

Hotel Terraza Amadores

Islas Afortunadas 1, Puerto Rico
Gran Canaria, Spain
Tel: +0034-928725613
Website: www.terrazadeamadores.com
Rate: $42+/ €31

The hotel is an apartment complex conveniently located in front of Playa Amadores Beach. Although it is close to the shopping area (only 300 meters from the nearest commercial center), it still retains its tranquil and peaceful atmosphere. Each apartment is clean and well maintained, and has a living room furnished with a sofa bed and a TV. It has a bathroom with private shower, and a kitchenette with a fridge, microwave oven, and coffee maker. Internet via modem is available in all public areas of the hotel for a surcharge. It offers great food and drinks at reasonable prices.

Riu Palace Maspalomas

Avda Tirajana s/n Playa del Ingles, Maspalomas
San Bartolome de Tirajana
35100 Spain
Tel: +34928769800
Rate: $83+/ €61

The hotel is situated close to Maspalomas Beach and the sand dunes. It is designed with colonial-style architecture much like a huge Roman amphitheater. It is near Yumbo shopping center and other attractions such as the Palmitos Park and Amadores Beach. The air-conditioned rooms open to balconies or terraces and are equipped with amenities, which include a private bathroom, telephone, mini-bar, and a satellite TV. It is located 30 kilometers from the airport, and 50 meters from the nearest bus stop. It has an outdoor pool, a sauna and a Jacuzzi. The hotel restaurant serves a variety of delicious food for both vegetarians and meat lovers alike.

Eating & Drinking

Restaurante La Tapita-Los Jose's, Maspalomas

Placido Domingo 12, Maspalomas
Gran Canaria, Spain
Tel: +34 928769680

The restaurant serves quality tapas at reasonable prices. There is a wide selection, which includes salad, tortilla, grilled Canarian cheese and a variety of meat, vegetarian and seafood dishes. The house wine is good and the service is excellent.

Mama Mia, Playa del Ingles

Centro Commercial Yumbo, Lower Floor
35100 Playa del Ingles
Gran Canaria, Spain
Tel: +34 633346899
www.mammamiagrancanaria.com

Mamma Mia is an Italian restaurant in the Yumbo Center. They serve authentic, classic Italian food, complete with primo and secondi items.

La Oliva, Las Palmas

c/Prudencio Morales 17
35009 Las Palmas de Gran Canaria
Gran Canaria, Spain
Tel: +34 928469757

La Oliva is a very busy and crowded restaurant known for its delicious tapas. The seafood dishes are superb, especially their fried calamari. The service is great and the prices are very reasonable.

Amadores Beach Club Restaurant, Puerto Rico

Playa Amadores, Puerto Rico
Gran Canaria, Spain

The menu is varied with a lot of fusion type meals, from seafood to steaks, to sushi and Mexican dishes, all at reasonable prices. It is a great location to watch the sunset, while enjoying your meal.

Fusion Restaurant & Lounge Bar, Arguineguin

Calle Alonzo Quesada 13, 35120 Arguineguin
Gran Canaria, Spain
Tel: +34 926185662
www.fusionrestaurantandloungebar.com

Fusion has delicious food and a soothing, relaxing ambiance. Fusion serves Asian food and you will enjoy favorites such as Pad Thai, hot and spicy soup, ginger chicken with pak choi, bang bang fish and ribs three way, as well as curries, salads and a variety of desserts. They have good value lunchtime specials. The staff are friendly and the restaurant is well worth a visit.

Shopping

Calle Mayor de Triana, Las Palmas

This pedestrian street is lined with stylish upmarket outlets as well as smaller shops selling local goods. You will find everything from exclusive boutiques to Indian bazaars. There are lots of retail clothing and shoe shops with attractive prices and there are plenty of cafes to refresh tired shoppers.

El Muelle Shopping Center (Centro Commercial El Muelle)

Muelle de Santa Catalina s/n
35008 Las Palmas de Gran Canaria
Gran Canaria, Spain
Tel: +34928327527

El Muelle shopping center is considered one of the best shopping centers in Spain. It is located inside the harbor near Parque Santa Catalina. It has 60 shops including clothing shops, such as Zara, Mango, Barshka, Benetton, and Massimo Dutti. There are shoe shops selling shoes "to die for", handbag shops selling leather bags and cases, costume jewelry shops, perfume shops, sports shops, and many more. Catch the number 40 bus, get off at Parque Santa Catalina, and take the lift to the ground floor – that's the easiest way to El Muelle.

Avenida Mesa y Lopez, Las Palmas

Avenida Mesa y Lopez is a shopping street near to the Parque Santa Catalina in Las Palmas and the street is lined with beautiful trees and shops. All the major chain stores in Spain are here including El Corte Ingles, the largest department store in the country. Marks & Spencers is also here. There are benches in the middle of the street where you can eat a picnic lunch before starting your next shopping spree.

FEDAC, Playa del Ingles

Cnr. Avenida Espana & Avenida EE UU, Playa del Ingles
Centro Insular del Turismo
Gran Canaria, Spain
Tel: +34928772445

If you are looking for local handicrafts, FEDAC is the place for you. It is a government sponsored, non-profit shop, where you can buy souvenirs at discounted prices.

Pueblo Canario (Canarian Village)

Parque Doramas
Las Palmas de Gran Canaria, 35005
Gran Canaria, Spain
Tel: +34 928242985
www.pueblocanarop.es/

The brothers Nestor and Miguel Martin Fernandez de la Torre built Pueblo Canario to preserve a site dedicated to Canarian culture. The buildings inside the village are designed in traditional Canarian architecture. Besides restaurants and a chapel, there are many handicraft shops where you can buy souvenirs and gifts.

GRAN CANARIA TRAVEL GUIDE

Printed in Great Britain
by Amazon